The
Angels' Trumpets

Alexandra The Great

PURPLE UNICORN MEDIA

Published by Purple Unicorn Media

ISBN 978-1-910718-12-4

Author Photograph by Rhiannon Guarino

PURPLE UNICORN MEDIA

Author's Note

The body of work in this book is meant to represent the journey of life: from birth where everything seems so fresh and innocent, to the coming of age or otherwise one's prime, where a person adapts the belief that love and danger are the most vital experiences, and that they are impervious to harm, then transitioning into adulthood, where the meaning of life is explored in depth, and it is often discovered that the closer one looks, the less they truly understand about themselves, then comes the golden age, where fate becomes more easily accepted as the person steps aside gradually to make way for the next generation, and finally, the cycle comes full circle with death.

Life is beautiful, because it is fleeting, and that must be remembered in the days to come. A person is the sum of their experiences and memories. Without them, they are nothing more than matter taking up space. This compilation is titled, The Angels' Trumpets, for a few different reasons. Angel Trumpets are beautiful flowers, but poisonous if consumed. They are an excellent representation of life; delicate, miraculous, wonderful, curious, euphoric, seductive, but deadly. The reader should plunge unconsciously into their psyche, and speculate the purpose of life like they never have before. Hopefully, they will come to appreciate, if they hadn't before, the small intricacies that make their own personal quest a unique, and blessed one, regardless of the trials and tribulations that plague each, and every soul along their way.

Thank you, and good luck,
Alexandra The Great

The Angels' Trumpets

The Score:

Chapter 1- The Prelude:
Began
Speak Easy in the Heart
Personal Declaration of Independence
Fearless
Next Seedling
My Kings

Chapter 2- The Movement:
In a Swallow's Heartbeat
Currents
Just an Understatement
Prime
Patients
Language
Dog's Plea
The Movement

Chapter 3- The Reprise:
The Majestic Mother
Head in the Sky
Birth Defect
Passion
When I Look Away
Of Dreams and Nightmares

Chapter 4- The Cadence:
Star Gazing
All Natural
Isolated
The Dancer
Death Before Life

Chapter 5- The Coda:
Matter That Never Was Flow
The Color of a Soldier
Honor
Unexpected
At My Funeral

The Angels' Trumpets

"Where the bright seraphim in burning row
Their loud uplifted angel trumpets blow"

John Milton

For Rojean, and Helen,
the women who have chased away
the hungry shadows
when I close my eyes at night

The Prelude

Began

You begin
your journey
pushing through a canal
that you won't remember,
and you can't see, but you are here
in the flesh;
one in six billion,
statistically speaking.

They give you a name.
They give you a number.
Your name can change.
Your number stays the same.
You are already in a hurry,
already running late.
They can't wait for you to walk,
then to talk,
go to school,
graduate,
procreate,
etc.

They teach what they're taught, a
little skewed,
a bit off.
Spongey hands absorb,
hungry eyes see us with
a smoking gun,
a hot head,
a drunken tongue,
an act of violence;
told to be pious.

Do as I say, not as I do,
"Hey you!"
They scream,
"You aren't supposed to be in there!"

but you weren't told it was ok
to be anywhere except your room,
your desk,
your chair.

You become uncertain of the world,
your role,
Ordinary, average, unique, exceptional
are the definitions you try to fit into
like geometric shapes,
but a circle won't go into a square.

Then you meet someone
who agrees that your
circle fits in her square.
You do things together
until you realize
you don't like those same things anymore.
Differences distract,
and life takes you by the hand,
"That was the wrong way, but we let's try
again."

You are never sure what this is all for,
but you try to define it,
put a title on it,
like they do you
with a number
and a name,
a definition,
and a game
to determine
your purpose,
test your brain,

ticks like a grandfather clock
ever analyzing,
ever changing hands,
ever moving in a circle,
that's starts at 12 o'clock,
and ends where it
began.

Speak Easy in the Heart

When mixing the oils
to produce a child of the revolution
onto naked canvas
with a jaded mind
and spliced ideals,
did Picasso
turn to Monet
and ask,
"What's the prompt?"

Personal Declaration of Independence

He sat
without flinching
from his desk.
The plastic remained
warm beneath his khakis.
His back, arched like an oak tree,
determined to glue
itself to the chair.

He waged war
against the teachers.
George Washington bared
the wood of his teeth
from his portrait hung
above the flag.

The principal showed
the bare of his arms as he
rolled up his sleeves,
ready to execute proper discipline.

They threw grenades,
rearing from their hands
to their hearts.

Mrs. Lynch echoed,
"You cannot have liberty,
if you do not stand and pledge,"
as if Liberty was the girl he would marry.
She could not trust him if he did not pledge.

The rain covered the windows
like plastic wrap,
beating the tin roof like
Chinese gongs,
but all he heard was his heart
breaking from its cage.
He distracted himself,
looking down at his shoes,
carefully counting the specks of mud

without standing.

When he did stand it was for the bell,
and he stood first.
So estranged, he was,
that no one moved before
he left the classroom.

A block from his house
he lost two teeth.
Bullies hung
him from the flag pole,
by his trousers,
squeezing him like a ripe pimple,
demanding answers,
"Why didn't you stand?!".
No one found out why he wouldn't rise.

All we know is that he was free
without declaring liberty.

Fearless

A crowd of foliage gathered,
and bled neutrals over the ground,
encouraging grass,
soothing the uneasy soil.

Vines entangled the Earth
embracing in a hug,
thanking it like
a spider thanks its prey.

Whispers flowed
between air pockets
of willows,
each where
a breath begins and ends.

The People came
in tremendous herds.
Their beasts ate half the grass.
The other half was plucked
like hairs on heads,
made from it their desires,
justifying their murders.

The People came,
and built from the loins of the forest;
built higher in an attempt to reach
the sun.

The People came,
and plants of power went up. Smoke
exhaled through
the community of nature,
turning up edges of the deadwood.
The People thrived with black
seeping from their
skin, and breathing almost nothing.

The soldiers stood
despite man,
however few in numbers.
But the People deemed them weak,
for they never budged
to revolt against their massacres,
they couldn't see the courage of
their stoic stance,
their arched backs.

Took their whispers for tears,
the People did,
but the wood was merely
discussing their reign once
humanity
came to an end.

Next

The sweat off your glass at the bar,
the way hair shines in fluorescent light,
the way you feel alive in the morning,
the way you feel with the presence of death at night,
the cold wind when your hot,
the waterfall of goosebumps that follows,
a friendly hug, when appropriate,
a strenuous hug that'd been neglected so long,
the tears born from an overdue reunion,
the feeling of time tumbling backwards,
the sharp anticipation,
the dull ting of routine,
all this we miss,
and cling only to let go
to let the next hit us,
like a jolt of a roller coaster,
with only one lingering
anchor
sinking our heights,
it will be over.

Whether
heaven, or, hell, or nothing,
or next lives, or purgatory
it isn't.
Now,
here,
at home.

Seedling

The wisest man in the world
wrote of the past everyday,
but could not correlate it with
the future.

A young boy sat next to him by
an oak tree three stories high
and many more stories old.

The boy asked,
"Where do we go when we die?"

He answered,
"You know better than I,
for you are closer to the point
in which there is no life."

My Kings

He sat with construction sweat and dirt
creating a formula in his hair
twining round the thin particles
and dividing itself among layers,
like threads of chocolate
running through a vanilla cake,
but much less sweet.

I sat on his lap,
and held his beer without drinking it;
just staring at the label,
and wondering what all those words meant,
wondering why he wanted another
and another,
how he grew more careless each time
the can fizzled,
and his lips sucked in
clear, yellow poison.

I smiled.
They spoke things I didn't understand,
that they wouldn't explain to me,
but I laughed, because of the way
their faces scrunched,
and their eyes squinted when they
said those things.

I was carried on
these dreams,
tethered like lily pads,
thinking I wanted to be like them;
rugged men,
wearing shirts with more holes
than a gopher could make in his life,
and stains more oppressive than
the odor of urine,
grinning with less teeth than I had yet to
grow, real men,
mature persons,
who knew some secret

of life from age that I did not have.
I felt a curiosity like wanting to flip
to the end of the book,
just to read the final paragraph.

They were so cool
reclining on patio furniture,
with red, white, and blue cans scattered
like flags,
and Frisbees flung where I couldn't catch
them; smoking these things that made
the air foggy and my throat sore.
They were my kings.

Now life has led
me down a winding, narrow path to destiny.
I'm walking barefoot holding my arms out,
smiling when I shouldn't be
for mere insanity.
I am waiting for it to rain.
The sky has been dark for so long,
like a corroded ceiling
ready to cave from the pressure.

At the end of the path, I see
myself in a nightie on his lap.
He is weathered like a hurricane.
He is dying,
and I'm sitting there laughing
at his jokes that were never funny.
I have become a thought.
a question,
a speculation in passing.

I have become what
I have learned to be.

The Movement

In a Swallow's Heart Beat

A culmination,
had arrived,
as if twelve instruments
weaved in and out of a pit;
producing harmonic ecstasy.
I believe they were fire bugs,
looking back.

There was a full moment,
not full as if we were stuffed from
a Thanksgiving dinner,
not full like the body of a Dominican cigar,
not full like the capacity of a crammed cell,
but full like the perfect bubble,
born amongst the dead ones,
round as a snowball
and lingering long after it
intercepted the ground.
This moment symbolized deliverance
of heart and bones to unfamiliar territory;
A spacious home presented cherished life
where they cranked up the ac,
and opened the windows at the same time.

We saw a type of love,
a new species in each others' eyes
like new colors had arose
inside their cores,
and as a caterpillar
wrapped in a cocoon,
the person changed first
on the inside,
their shell melted like
wax from the branch,
from the tree
to the dirt,
and our arms were no longer arms,

but wings.
We forgot the hindrance of
traveling on the ground.

We held each other
on nights where tears
set the stage,
weeping over barely ivory carpets,
cursing the world's name.

But it was music when it came together,
like stitches in a tie;
that reached passed our stomachs
to the floor.

Twelve instruments
belted out one long song
of one long journey across
the strain of summer hearts,
warm and real.

Currents

We watch Autumn's iced breath levitate leaves,
the crisp collision appeared to be a delicate waltz.
The breeze whisks strands
of rust and gold from your face,
careening them in currents that form
infinite curls that spire into
an imaginary wave splashing
into your smoldering footsteps.
Smoke rises from your lips
in a travesty to release me with 'goodbye'.
I forbid it's looming presence
from poisoning this virginal moment;
scorching the night with this fatal blow.
Your disappearance becomes my disillusion
at a current's end.

I fasten my heart around vague ideas,
that leak out of orifices,
attempting to bind you to my doorstep
with your doleful gaze and supple lips,
awaiting my right words
to exonerate them,
We'd revel the wind vortex
with a blistered kiss that catches fluctuation
of your soul, and adheres it to mine, effortlessly.
You're safe before dawn within my shadow.
I'd never let you drown in my eyes.

Just an Understatement

Summed up,
like a crossword puzzle's key,
I am one day
out of the nine thousand, nine hundred, and ninety six
I've experienced.

Now, I am my mother
tucking me into bed.
For an instance,
I see the sunrise in her eyes,
as brilliant as the first sunrise
that ever saw this Earth.

She and I,
are both the book, and the lamp on my desk,
both the medicine and the spoon.
I will make us equal,
by representing both of us.

The blankets that held me had tiny flowers.
I remember asking why they were smaller
than regular flowers.
She didn't know, but made up a reason.

My pajamas were made of fabric
that felt like your bathing suit bottom
after sitting on concrete.
They were green like my eyes,
like her eyes.
I pictured her wearing it and giggled.

That day, I knew who I was.
I was her daughter.
I was yet to smoke cigarettes,
skip school,
break men,
or learn what was hard about life
to be able to scribe something soft.

Her cheeks rose to the occasion.

I wanted to be her when I grew up,
as she stayed the same.
I believed in the impossible
like wishing on stars,
tossing coins into fountain,
and when I did,
that was what I wished for.

I am still that person,
I thought I'd be,
covering up lies with
whale blubber,
just as she.

Sometimes, when my heart
is scooped like a cucumber cup
ready to be filled with impurities,
I think of how mother would weasel
her way out of the pain,
like I'd weasel my way out of her
arms when being scolded.

I know who I am,
not by the damage incurred,
but from the faith
earned in a heart undeveloped.

Prime

She sees me, and she is me,
in her fragile mind,
strutting with failed maturity
like a knock-off hand bag on my arm.

For now,
she is six feet tall
with legs like a spider,
casting shadows across the parking lot.
Her hips sway
like choppy waves beat the shore,
unsteady, yet persistent.

One whiff of my perfume
morphs this rabid beast
into a tame creature purring gently,
as my footsteps synchronize her rapid breathing.

Her hands twist into a pretzel in her lap,
she waits for my signal,
and catches my step so that we are one.

When I fall back,
she pouts her lips, and scrunches her eyes
expecting them to be graced with makeup
when she opens them.
She shrinks back to seven in my absence.

She sees me, and she is me,
in her fragile mind,
hums Sinatra and rocks on her toes,
with visions of her prime,
turning her nose up at men,
as if she were the tender cut of steak unpierced,
yet displayed.

Words falter,
their failed vigil
hoists a white flag
across her blistered lips,

reluctantly surrendering to time and order.
Eyes chastise the hem of my skirt,
trimmed short from the trend of her day.

Her breath is fresh in my presence,
not stale like the distinct taste of dust at dawn,
and death in darkness.

With bold validity,
she envisions rising from her wheel chair
to flaunt her spider vein legs,
revolving like pistols,
playing Russian Roulette,
twirling pirouettes around me.

In my stead,
she slumps, and swallows meds,
kissing the horizon of her youth one last
time.
She clings to her prime within my eyes;
shrinks back to seventy in my absence.

Patients

Action is patience's spirit,
you must act, then wait.
Nothing comes of either
when one is done alone.

He who sits for his future,
dies in the waiting room.

Language

LETTERS
blot the white,
shuttering under
the notes
we pass across the universe.

The stains
are deep,
but depth is relative.
When the alphabet
is mixed with red sauce
it is, but noodle shapes swimming
in a vast sea of senselessness;
connecting only momentarily,
piercing reason
by joining the mouth.

Words,
all sizes and pronunciations,
stand tall,
proud of their singular definitions,
refining a small link
of understanding.
Words are deemed pointless,
when rambled
out of nursing homes
and sanitariums.

A syllable
can change everything,
making words into
weapons,
gifts,
lies,
love.
Language is the most pliable
material one purchases with their lips.
Words raise and drop
in continuous motion,
yet remain still.

They are tricksters,
hiding in multiple interpretations;
wielding tongue lashed swords.

L E T T E R S,
are words, words are sentences,
sentences are stories,
stories teach,
without knowledge
we are nothing more than apes.
No matter which way you build them,
you get the same conclusion;
communication is important as breath.

Nothing's gonna change my world.
Your words,
my words
will marry or divorce
condense or evaporate.
Let them thrive either way;
staining the page
for evolution's sake.

Dogs' Plea

Puppies behind a white fence
flay their tongues desperately,
pawing at the posts of the gate.
Barks roll into the streets
absorbed by undesired ears.

Hot chords divulge sound,
molded by the tongue,
expanded by the mouth,
deposited through the teeth.

A man in Haiti is shot
for what he said.
Blood pours through his teeth
like a leak in a dam.
A mother silences his daughter
with her words;
like a jungle cat;
licking the child's tears
consuming exposed fear.

The girl's father is dead.
He cannot speak.
The girl speaks instead,
the new politician in the family.
She lies with her lips
faster than rain pours.
She is the reassuring sunset.

A criminal walks.
Evidence is swallowed.
The tongue rattled
to be released from its' cage.
Shock morphed his
quivering lips into sponges
that collected his shameful
repudiation leaking like a dam
from his eyes,
and the pitiful sound
of barking rang clear.

A haunting visage resonates,
puppies behind a fence;
defenseless.
Let him free from his sins.
His tongue wags well.

A boy takes a stick,
and drags it along the boards,
smack, smack, smack.
He locks the gates,
and ignores the cries
of the dogs.
Only he is truly free.

The Movement

When the parlor door opened,
it wasn't heard,
floating over their heads like banana smoke,
but the looks came regardless,
taking bites out of places in our arms
as we passed,
chewing loudly, as if they hadn't been rude yet.
Bob Dylan was the music to set the scene,
but if the jukebox knew
it might have played louder;
filling the cockles of our hearts
with warm liquid sound.
Cinnamon coffee spilled down our shirts
as we swayed
away...

"How many roads must a man walk down
Before you call him a man?"

And they couldn't touch us.
We were emitting radiation
which burned to watch,
as the flower children
talked of demonstrations
and women's studies, addition to curriculum, and
birth control releasing like a freedom
to be obtained at a small price.
We decided not to have kids,
after all.

"The answer, my friend, is blowin' in the wind,
The answer is blowin' in the wind."

They whispered 'derelicts',
we shouted 'anti-bandwagon liberty'.
They pushed the word 'beat-nicks',
we replied 'beaten into submission'.
Their fathers made bombs with their hands,
and if our fathers did,
they weren't our fathers.

"Yes, 'n' how many times can a man turn his head,
Pretending he just doesn't see?"

At the mention of the LSD survey,
Becky with tie-dye knees highs
and orange braids
yelps and slides off her seat,
if this meant she wasn't
subject to the Pigs,
it might have been her saving grace,
but it was foolish
to think that shy Becky
with blue, and yellow braces,
was not subject to the Pigs
on the account of an accident.

"The answer, my friend, is blowin' in the wind,
The answer is blowin' in the wind"

They came at us like
criminals,
us
in peace bearing clothes
softly stirring with conformity's protest,
will not be one with the system,
will not be one with the skin.

The pigs squealed
wildly,
mechanically
rehearsing our rights,
and Becky spat on one,
clenching her braces
to look like a gremlin.

Our lives were
blowing in the wind,
so delicately,
that they dare disrupt them,
stealing a moment
like murdering a dandelion;
carelessly dismembering it

without consideration
to fate?

So they took us away,
committing a quadruple homicide on
our freedom,
each stain was like blood
upon the bar stools,
cascaded in tie-dye trails.
No one sat on them for days.

The Reprise

The Majestic Mother

Why call it a sunrise,
when it is the Earth
that rises to greet the Sun?

Gusts of pollution
pat my back,
as I wane over the edge.
Pebbles break free of their casing.
Landslides concave and curl inward toward the cliff,
hugging the barren existence.

The sky was filled
like the apple center of a pie,
beaming without distinct form,
just the color scheme fading back into black.
An expanding orb crashes into a spot of land,
and rumbles the earth some ninety two million miles away,
or so she seemed to intersect.

We are
leaning on her stellar beauty
supporting the weight of luscious lakes,
and billowing life.
Aware that if we toe the fragile line,
pushing the limits of her mercy,
she could swallow us whole,
flick us out of orbit
with her middle finger
adjacent to the planets.

Oh, how my eyes would swell
worth laying down my life
to witness the explosion.
Grains of glorious ash,
all that we know melts before us.

A cosmic craze

and haze of smoke and rock collapsing
beneath our legs.
Our fortresses built with dignity
reduced to sharpened pencils
beneath a bulldozer.

We float off in pieces without gravity,
like cookie crumbs disappear in a tub of milk.
Fragile records kept so precious
blow away like dust.
Who will care then?

I smile at the orb,
as if it were nodding at me
with approval.
Winking its sun spots,
brushing death in my face delicately,
as subtle as the breeze.

Head in the Sky

He feels the soil beneath his boots,
and knows there will be road.
The wet soil will be piled without end,
and paved, and repaved,
and painted, and driven,
and worn, and torn,
and left for one car
to ride it's stretch without
wondering what it once was, or could've
been.

He feels the footprints of tractors.
He knows the consistency of the soil, beneath
his fingertips,
and dreams of luxurious green.
Wrapping arms cross each other
in an embrace only a forest might
agree to.
The flowers would grow
between his toes.

The sun would filter through
his gray beard.
The dirt would perk up to see
him again,
after all these years of longing.

He smells the soil,
damp from an absent storm.
Fertile bellied molecules scream
to be seeded,
and he without growth to give.

He envisions
a burnt sun priming
the canvas of the land
with stalks, and crops,
and sprouts, and mounds
all primed for a feast
with only one guest.

Birth Defect

If love does not flourish
like vines
that hug the entrance
to a garden,
then children should
not erupt from it.
Seeds disperse from perishing trees,
that expect full bodied
specimen to mature,
half in shadow.

I am a product of those shadows,
having spotted love once,
but did not advance
for fear of falling
down that black, slippery corridor.

I am one of those children,
tortured by the concept of replication.

Just a weed among weeds
looking for a flower to thrive upon,
murdering the beautiful
with my groping for steadiness,
conceived from sputtering hearts.

Passion

I don't know you, and yet I need to speak to you,
when it is all there is left to do,

like a hot air balloon dropping sand in order to rise
I need altitude to survive.

I was once right on high,
thin bones memorizing keys.

A maddening calm fashioned me one day.
Focus slid from me, like sweat from a half empty glass,
and all I'd see is the bottom mimicking me
in a stand still.

And I fought for you, passion,
as a light house fights for a boat to save,
or a path wishes a soul to claim.
I prayed for you
till I realized you weren't a force,
but a tool.

A man is forever broken .
One must keep tuning the strings,
and rotating the engine.

The moments don't matter, but what you make of them
and are you wasting them,
wishing you were other parts and
better tools?

When you use distractions,
whether they be pleasures, suppressors, or fillers,
it is, because you are afraid of life.
You know the contract of life.
You want to believe it's no good,
yet deep down you know
there is nothing else you know,
and your legacy lies in all your doubts and fears.
So you run to stay the way

you are today.

I feeling nothing today,
and come to an agreement with tomorrow,
and leave my footprints for the next,
and hope that I taught those footprints to be free,
to live beyond my legacy,
and become something more than
the pleasures, suppressors, and fillers
ever allowed me to be.

When I Look Away

My mother is smiling at me
in black,
posted against white,
and who knows why she's smiling,
but I haven't seen it in so long.

Sometimes she's crying,
streaking crooked brooks
across a withered face
pulled taut like a rose
before bloom.

Every time she's standing
like an Empress
with a booming chest
engraved with stone,
that doesn't look heavy
from the angle she has curved herself,
a hunter cat at full attention.

She is smiling at me,
because I've pleased her,
written that novel
that I haven't plotted yet,
kissed her cheek
without using a receiver,
turned myself back
into a child that she could nurture
another eighteen years,
and she'd be happy
to wear the pain again
like a woolen shawl
itching her neck.

She smiles, because she has
a place, as "Mama",
not as Rojean, or
or ex-wife, or friend,
or acquaintance met
in a bar,

but one of permanence
like a statue
that will live in infamy,
that will withstand
the frowns for one more smile.

Mother is without color
in my mind, except her cheeks.
as pink as apricots in summer.

She is worn from life,
like shingles on a roof,
but when I see her in my mind
she is more grand than you or I,
sometimes standing at a podium
giving lectures
to students.
She is wise,
donning that constant smile
more potent than death.

She gives me hope
to return to the minutes,
and face the hours.
She laughs at me;
tells me to stop daydreaming,
there will be achievements
to smile for later.

Of Dreams and Nightmares

Every little nothing has led me to today,
the point where the past and future intersect,
like smeared pigments of a rainbow combine
to paint reality,
but it is translucent and fading,
brilliant, yet empty.
My attempts at pursuing the purpose of this rainbow
are as successful as catching a tornado.
My time is either bought or sold.
Who really knows?

I have been lazy for my belief in fate.
I have been busy in my search for self-determination.
I have become dismal while spinning in circles,
and throwing my head back,
squinting for a smile to smack me like a sun beam;
to bless me with relief under my God,
but grew dizzy too quickly.
I have felt ashamed when I hadn't prayed.
I have felt naive when I took to my knees,
and held my own hands next to my night coffin,
as I confided in the ground or the walls
to satisfy my soul despite perceived insanity.

I have tossed coins into fountains;
as if donating to fund the realization of my dreams.
I have been a skeptic of salvation,
and a firm believer of nothing,
while waiting for an epiphany
to calm my quivering bones that don't know.
I have been thirsty for knowledge.
I have been drunk on doubt.

I have ridiculed the warriors who took their lives
before they were stolen from them.
I have envied the saps who breathed in bullets instead of air.
I have vowed that love will save us all.
I have sworn off love prior to taking the fall.
I have been cynical about apathy,
apathetic about cynicism.

I have been afraid of nothing.
I have been afraid to admit that the thought
of nothing terrifies me.
I have protested with unwavering conviction.
I have been silent; brimming with indecision.
I have been yesterday.
I will be tomorrow.

I am today;
a conundrum,
a contradiction,
an example of dramatic irony,
and may at least the audience find humor in my tragedy. Maybe they
can make sense of all this devastation.
Maybe their puzzle came with all the proper pieces.
Maybe they can put their lives in order,
and pretend that doing so makes them whole,
but as for me I am blurry, and unrecognizable,
when I look into the glass,
and swallow the reversed reflection of me.

All this experience, and time invested,
and accumulated knowledge
amounts to the admission of,
"I don't know. I'll never know,"
but keep searching anyway,
smitten with idealism,
consumed by confusion,
and lost in desperation,
happily.

The Cadence

Star Gazing

An omniscient alien,
pulls from within,
without my consent.
It hovers above, curious,
monitoring human interaction,
smashing into one another
like bumper cars,
like bowling balls smack gutter rails,
for result of impact.

They test pain's pact,
"You will feel alive, as you die,
you will feel alive again, as you collide.
From birth you've been peaking at demise,
yet hesitant to startle its' restless eye."

Mankind wages war,
to say that they fought,
for the right reasons, or not.
Bodies induce war,
to say that love was made,
whether skin friction or destiny.
Political figures seek war,
modern prophets;
save souls, or save face.

Self-proclaimed stars,
shed freckles of light
over sunblock-ed pores,
to relate or captivate;
seems sufficient
to fuel subliminal addictions,
until we outgrow their emotional burdens,
syndicate their rifts,
before burying them amongst kin,
lyrics stale,
like flavorless gum,

rubber putty grazes the tongue.
Spit it out, and search for a new stick of song,
to chew on.

They say this man star is dead today,
but my omniscient friend,
is not convinced,
because suddenly amnesia of the lips
is cured, rehearsing those distant odes again,
waiting for the play to begin.
Unable to catch the ghost
in the quest for unanswered questions,
millions mourn murdered strangers,
bustling like life guards
resuscitating flood victims,
far too late.

Maybe vicariously,
people clutch their hearts,
layering armor to protect the caged.
Their trepidations,
more likely for their own mortality,
pour like thick smoke
into congested throats,
that realize fate is not a fairy,
if our stars don't recognize forever.

Since sight and sound
are our affirmations,
we talk and talk
about these legends,
as if voices could rise
decaying bones,
that may someday return
the favor.

How ironic that one's end,
should proceed their victory,
that absent of breath the masses
commiserate and connect only then,
like star gazers ask
the ancient sky for advice
blazing knowledge,

shed eons ago, reciprocates
like skin coats aglow, striped
before eyes could savor such truth.

All Natural

There is no blame in nature.
Fleeting, rocks grapple with a cliff,
before barreling down like mice.

Where is the fault?

An apple is already ruined.
When she grows she is bound
to the supple grass,
like a baby's crib,
cradling her fall.
She impregnates the Earth,
unity comes quickly,
painless.

Opposites reign,
fire ignites hay stacks,
while cackling brooks
indecently overlook the incident.

Opposites thrive
in the fortitude of trees,
provoking fear with a wave
of their branched leaves.
Bushes populate fields,
supple and curious,
but unsuspecting thorns
protect their ominous beauty.

We are all a composition of opposites;
light, and dark, and born doomed.

Weak as brittle leaves,
with hardly a limb to hold,
we sustain.
Vantage points are skewed
by blame, so diverse it is difficult
to see a prominent cycle.
Opposites were never at fault.

We are in our winter.
It is bleak within our minds,
and more piercing still outside,
when the ice freezes over
predictability.

Isolated

Alone within myself,
I speak into oblivion.
No one comprehends,
but some muster a,
"How do you do?" or "How are you?"
It all equivocates the same,

'I don't care, but tell me anyways.'
Tell me about your day.
Tell me how the sky experienced you,
and how he took your parking spot.

I can't relate to those moments,
because I am me,
and you are you.

We are steadfast brooks
passing over rocks, so intimately,
yet without notice.

We brush each other
more closely
than words can relate,
yet we are isolated,
with selfish thoughts
of where we go,
instead of where we are.

I am within a bookstore.
I interpret according
to the shape of what I see.
I see you Elliot and Edgar,
with brutal eyes I study your insides.
I receive an "A" on
your composure,
but surely
an incomplete on your intentions.

We try to show what we mean,
but do you even understand me, when

I tell you that I am isolated?
It is fresh with vomited definition
I can't begin to explain.

So existentialism,
is smashed in the face of you and I.

I see it for a block of brick,
I can't obstruct.

You see it as a bubble,
you can't pop.

Is it not true that we both
do see it?

Should I believe myself,
or your riddled off lies?

You save face, requesting of me,
"How are you?"
eyes brimming with unwept tears.

"I'm fine, just peachy",
devastation lingering,
behind the dismissed
blink of an eye.

The Dancer

I saw her battle to be positive
from the passenger's seat of her van,
As she assembled strength
from a place other than from within her frail,
debilitating frame,
though the photo
beneath the frame,
gleamed brighter than light allowed.

She spoke of intangible life,
when the body's will has ceased.
I chose not to speak.
My conscience would not deter her from her
ideals.
Who was I to steal them?
Only death should perform that awful deed.

Dismally, I watched
the lines lacerate her once pristine face.
Reality had already planted its' wicked seed,
and if I tried to dig out the weed,
it might ensue fatality.
As my mother's audience, I sat helpless
to prevent the world from clawing at her
with tiger paws.
Forever in debt to her, I am,
and forever I shall be.
I must come to grips
with time's anomaly.

Yet even now,
A ripe seventy, she held her head high, stretched
her back like a cat,
and peered down her glass rimmed nose at me,
to inspect the product of her genes;
the harvest of her family tree.

Forcing a coral smile,
she gave me something to
envision as we barreled down I4,

"I decided to dance, once a day, every day,"
she continued to explain,
"I loved to dance, when I was your age.
It makes me happy, it's also great exercise.
Maybe I'll fit into my old bathing suit
next summer!"
My eyes lit up,
as she danced around the four by four space,
she cleared to make her debut in the living room of her trailer,
Sinatra swaying in place of her would be partner.

It was magical.
I would try to keep her there,
in the vault of my mind,
my mother, the dancer, the dreamer, the fighter, the believer,
and suddenly life didn't seem so dreadful.

Death Before Life

In that time between,
when winter pecks the windows,
and spring tarries like a preying hock
perched atop trees, is where you'll find me.
No one speaks to cut the ice
that cakes the sidewalks.

I am lying still.
I am still lying.

He comes to me, with a word of advice,
my pretty bird from his lofty height,
but he doesn't remember my name.
The frost cracks, but does not part.

Gaping at the morning sun,
I trickle like a slushy.
The rays lick me, like a thousand tongues,
I will not melt for.
The wind beats me, like a welcome rug,
I will not bend for.
The grass beneath me is my lover.
I have smothered him.
Wretched are my kisses,
fornicating with his gentle core,
until his smooth stem breaks like a twig.

The bird sings to me once more,
urges my frigid nature to subside, before
the thirsty sun arrives.

I am helpless, as the frost,
believing myself invincible,
when I'm not.

Echoes reverberate the entire field.
I do not move an inch.
Spring is comin' like a freight train.
Spring is comin' like a baby boy.
Spring is soarin' like the horizon.

I'll only catch a glimpse of its sublimity
before mortality summons.

I cry aloud.
I'm allowed to cry.

Love
is in the atoms
shaving the ice.

Flurries of dawn fall over the ground.
I rake in the gale of laughter with luster,
like a new day that will be everlasting.
I won't be present.

I'm fine with that.

My vigor will rescind when I am lifted.
Frost will be unthinkable for seasons to
come.

I can only hope
the grass will grow while
the song bird forgets my name.

The Coda

Matter That Never Was

Goodbye is a stillborn
evading life before we
knew its purpose.

Flow

Now that the garden
is closed,
where store left over time?
The jaded sky
mourns for vines, grappling
like neglected infants
suckling the Earth's teat.

I watch my Eden
decay like a forfeited field,
hoisting a white flag
on the eve of a battle.
Flower buds are too wise to bloom.
Blood will soon rape them.
I empathize with the pile of leaves
waiting for that final rake
to deplete them of oxygen.

Keeping bones busy,
the foliage survives
like wounded soldiers,
and I, their crippled medic.
They blush at the attendance of
sunlight; breaking between gaps in the
fence.
Poppies tentatively peak,
like curious sea shells inspect the shore
before they slip back into their salty
graves.

What now?
Watch my green apprentices wither
through snow flaked glass?
Whisper my farewells,
and hope like a mother lioness,
sending her cubs into the wilderness,
that we'll reunite next Spring?
Or suggest life to the deceased,
with, but a waning smile
and stained gloves to offer respite?

Their eyes spare courage for only me.

I will take a yellow pill,
escorted by a red, followed by a blue
to maintain like the garden,
till the certainty of Winter engulfs.

My fledglings
will endure the snow, and wind.
They represent eternity.
Someday, they will
weed out the evils of this world,
and my grave will rest at peace in
their presence.

I plant the futures' seeds in empty
pots despite the sufferance
of my own thin rewards.

The Color of a Soldier

Each soldier's outline was distinct
as crayons lining a box.
Each represented an emblem
smuggled into the army,
bedecked with decals beneath their uniforms,
patches of soul tattooed over hearts.
Bright faces blanched with duties
they shouldn't have claimed,
inheriting the outcome
of political disputes,
while the 'influential'
placed bets behind the lines.

Bombastic thoughts
came second to the compressed tension
swelling inside the jet plane,
adding excess weight
to their backpacks.

The boys prepared their feet to depart
solid ground,
spouting out wills to their comrades in case,
well, just in case.

Each soldier plummeted through the clouds
with empty dreams,
still heavier than anticipated,
strapped to their backs.
A rainbow spilled into the sky.

Visions of home overwhelmed minds,
flashing faster than they fell.
The flag was irrelevant,
seemed so very far from the cold sky.
Red, white, and blue
could not parallel their thoughts,
their aspirations,
took an opposite route
from their destinations.

No room,
for precious moments,
shared memories in combat.

Bodies were numbers,
not colors.
Few survived,
paled and retreated,
hung out to dry a stark white.

The reverent and glistening sky adorned
fresh minds
that were painted one color upon their
arrival, and green became crimson red,
amen.

Honor

They stretched the flag over his casket
should it keep him protected,
through the trenches beyond.
This was the tradition used
to honor a fallen hero,
another mans' murderer,
Uncle Sam's son,
or the remains of an orphan's father.

Twenty one guns wailed the loudest.
Their sound drown out the voices of everyone,
having loved the man more deeply,
than he ever intended to be loved.
Loaded within their chambers
were secrets his grave would not uphold.

Later people will say,
because they believe they should,
that his service was dignified and true.
Each soldier stood to carry him,
since he no longer could.
Before this day we would've bet,
he'd stay a stone among us,
while the Earth swallowed us whole,
but now we know.

The breeze stirred changing leaves,
as an eerie reminder to our restless souls.
It snickered, as we savored precious dregs of time,
hesitantly sipped upon as if the finest wine.
Glad we were, at least today,
to be sticks instead of stones.

As his chapter closed,
I felt no resolution,
viewed no apparent honor,
though certain it was implied,
no resolve in this routine salute,
no closure in our empty "goodbyes".
There was no rapture here to claim his soul.
Only the guns did mourn,
where unfocused eyes remained dry.

Unexpected

I felt the day
as soft as a grand number
of feathers lain flat
covered with triple
layered silk reducing to
an oval shape.

I felt the morning
dripping emissaries
of dew onto my forehead.
Granules were tentative
like ballroom dancing
trading positions,
but never exiting.

I felt the air
it was just cool
enough to wear a jacket,
or go naked.
The pollen made my nose
flinch like a rabbit.

It was cloudless
and hapless.
It was the consistency
of every day of the year
mixed till frothy,
then boiled at high temperatures,
left to sizzle down in the fridge.

I saw squirrels
frenzying with no destination
through the maze of tawny leaves
the wind taming their hair
in a fickle manner.

I saw the sky
a blue canvas
with endless accord
the small intricacies

moving against it
introducing life
to otherwise spectacular
dead.

My face was warm
in the sunlight,
feet were divorced
from the heat
I held like black concrete
does.

I felt the intentions
of the light,
like minced, gold plated
furniture, carpet
and skin
wherever happened in.

I heard the doorbell.
Upon opening I discovered
it was Death.

"How could you visit
today? Let me see
your schedule!?"

Sure enough in crimson
ink my name at the top.
I argued
that today was too perfect.
God set it up this way.
All looks to want to be touched.
I must see everything,
experience everything
that the day has to offer.

He extended his arm to me.
I beckoned like a child
obeying their mother.
He lead me to something
far less beautiful.

At My Funeral

If there is a God,
He would be the only one
with something meaningful to say
at my funeral.

I see
those know-less souls
standing in a crescent,
holding hands,
like branches hold
dead leaves,
and swaying evermore gently.

They'd say things
that are more for their image,
than my severance.

"Oh dear, she was a blessing,"
teary eyed, but blank faced,
"She loved animals.
She was so modest,
always told me *I* was great.
We will miss her so.
Oh whoa..."

But God would stand
with a chunk missing from His hip,
and say that I was that hole in Him.

People in bow ties
choking at their necks
will stand here, and stand there;
pushing complicated dishes
in simple peoples' face.
There will be music,
and merriment.
The pillow will be
just as soft for them tonight;
as soft as my breath
will break from my

darkest night.

God will only mourn.

God never sleeps
when his children are in need.

That is why I search my bones,
chip away at this tender soul
like a piece of raw meat,
my own delicacy,
for some proof that
at my funeral
something will be there
to take care
of the remains
of the soul.

www.ingramcontent.com/pod-product-compliance
Lightning Source LLC
Chambersburg PA
CBHW060537030426
42337CB00021B/4317